Houghton
Mifflin
Harcourt

JOURNEYS
COMMON CORE

Program Authors

James F. Baumann · David J. Chard · Jamal Cooks
J. David Cooper · Russell Gersten · Marjorie Lipson
Lesley Mandel Morrow · John J. Pikulski · Héctor H. Rivera
Mabel Rivera · Shane Templeton · Sheila W. Valencia
Catherine Valentino · MaryEllen Vogt

Consulting Author

Irene Fountas

Unit 5

Watch Us Grow

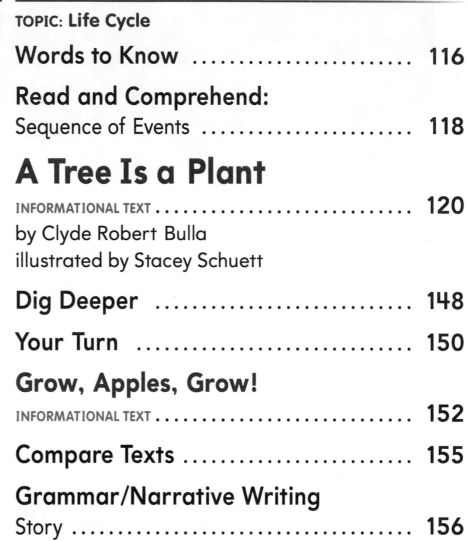

Welcome, Reader!

What happens to living things as they grow? That's what the stories in this book are about. You will meet animals and children who are learning new things. You will even meet a funny toad who wonders if singing songs and telling stories will help his garden seeds grow.

As you read, the number of words you know grows, too! Read on!

Sincerely,

The Authors

unit 5

☑ **WORDS TO KNOW**
High-Frequency Words

few

night

loudly

window

noise

story

shall

world

Vocabulary Reader

Context Cards

Words to Know

▶ Read each **Context Card.**

▶ Choose two blue words. Use them in sentences.

1 **few**
There are only a **few** trees here.

2 **night**
The buds open in the day and close at **night.**

3 loudly

The bird sang loudly in the tree.

4 window

The big tree is very close to the window.

5 noise

I heard a noise in the garden.

6 story

He tells a story about planting trees.

7 shall

We shall pick apples today.

8 world

My garden is the best place in the world.

Read and Comprehend

☑ **TARGET SKILL**

Story Structure The parts of a story work together. **Characters** are the people and animals. The **setting** is when and where a story takes place. Events make up the **plot**. The plot is often about a problem and how characters solve it. A story map can help you tell about the different parts.

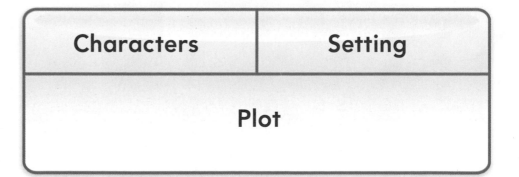

Characters	Setting
Plot	

☑ **TARGET STRATEGY**

Analyze/Evaluate Tell how you think and feel about the story. Use text evidence to tell why.

COMMON CORE

RL.1.3 describe characters, settings, and major events; **RL.1.7** use illustrations and details to describe characters, setting, or events

To make a garden grow, you start with seeds. You plant them in the soil. Then you take care of them. You make sure they have enough water and sunlight. Soon, the seeds will start to grow. Tiny plants will pop up in the soil. They will get bigger. Soon you will have big plants with flowers or vegetables.

Next, you will read a story about what happens when a character named Toad plants some seeds in **The Garden**.

ANCHOR TEXT

ARNOLD LOBEL
Frog and Toad Together

✅ TARGET SKILL

Story Structure Tell about the characters, setting, and events in a story.

✅ GENRE

A **fantasy** is a story that could not happen in real life. Look for:

▶ animals who talk and act like people

▶ events that could not really happen

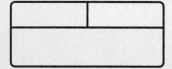

COMMON CORE **RL.1.3** describe characters, settings, and major events; **RL.1.7** use illustrations and details to describe characters, setting, or events; **RL.1.10** read prose and poetry

Meet the Author and Illustrator

Arnold Lobel

Arnold Lobel started drawing when he was a child. When he grew up, he wrote and illustrated almost 100 books for children. His books won many awards. Frog and Toad have even been in a Broadway musical!

The Garden

from Frog and Toad Together

by Arnold Lobel

Frog was in his garden.

Toad came walking by.

"What a fine garden you have, Frog,"

he said.

"Yes," said Frog. "It is very nice,

but it was hard work."

"I wish I had a garden," said Toad.

"Here are some flower seeds.

Plant them in the ground," said Frog,

"and soon you will have a garden."

"How soon?" asked Toad.

"Quite soon," said Frog.

Toad ran home.

He planted the flower seeds.

"Now seeds," said Toad, "start growing."

Toad walked up and down a few times.

The seeds did not start to grow.

Toad put his head
close to the ground
and said loudly,
"Now seeds, start growing!"
Toad looked at the ground again.
The seeds did not start to grow.

Toad put his head
very close to the ground
and shouted,
"NOW SEEDS, START GROWING!"
Frog came running up the path.
"What is all this noise?" he asked.
"My seeds will not grow," said Toad.
"You are shouting too much," said Frog.
"These poor seeds are afraid to grow."
"My seeds are afraid to grow?" asked Toad.

ANALYZE THE TEXT

Repetition What words are
repeated on these pages? Why?

"Of course," said Frog.

"Leave them alone for a few days.

Let the sun shine on them,

let the rain fall on them.

Soon your seeds will start to grow."

That night
Toad looked out of his window.
"Drat!" said Toad.
"My seeds have not
started to grow.
They must be afraid of the dark."
Toad went out to his garden
with some candles.
"I will read the seeds a story,"
said Toad.
"Then they will not be afraid."
Toad read a long story to his seeds.

ANALYZE THE TEXT

Story Structure What is Toad's problem? How is he trying to solve it?

All the next day
Toad sang songs
to his seeds.

And all the next day
Toad read poems
to his seeds.

And all the next day
Toad played music
for his seeds.

Toad looked at the ground.
The seeds still did not
start to grow.
"What shall I do?" cried Toad.
"These must be
the most frightened seeds
in the whole world!"

Then Toad felt very tired,
and he fell asleep.

"Toad, Toad, wake up," said Frog.
"Look at your garden!"
Toad looked at his garden.
Little green plants were coming up
out of the ground.

"At last," shouted Toad,
"my seeds have stopped
being afraid to grow!"
"And now you will have
a nice garden too," said Frog.

"Yes," said Toad,
"but you were right, Frog.
It was very hard work."

Dig Deeper

How to Analyze the Text

Use these pages to learn about Story Structure and Repetition. Then read **The Garden** again.

Story Structure

Frog and Toad are the **characters** in **The Garden**. What kind of place is the **setting** of this story? Does the story happen during the day, at night, or both? Think about the problem Toad has and how it is solved. Use a story map to write text evidence about the characters, setting, and important events.

Characters	Setting
Plot	

RL.1.3 describe characters, settings, and major events; **RL.1.7** use illustrations and details to describe characters, setting, or events

Repetition

Authors sometimes use the same words or same kind of event over and over in a story. This is called **repetition**. This can make the story fun to read. It can also help you understand what is important in the story.

Look at page 24. What does Toad do over and over? Why do you think the author uses the words **all the next day** more than once?

Your Turn

 my WriteSmart

RETURN TO THE ESSENTIAL QUESTION

 Turn and Talk

What grows in a garden? Talk with a small group. Then talk about the problem Toad has when he tries to grow his garden. How is it solved? Use details from text evidence to explain your ideas and feelings clearly.

Classroom Conversation

Talk about these questions with your class.

1. Describe what Toad does to get his seeds to grow. What really makes them grow?

2. How does Frog help Toad?

3. What would you plant in a garden? How would you take care of the garden?

Response Write a book report about **The Garden**. Begin by telling the name of the story and what it is mainly about. Then tell what you like about it. Give reasons why. Tell what you don't like. Give reasons why.

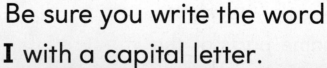

Writing Tip

Be sure you write the word **I** with a capital letter.

COMMON CORE

RL.1.1 ask and answer questions about key details; **RL.1.3** describe characters, settings, and major events; **RL.1.7** use illustrations and details to describe characters, setting, or events; **W.1.1** write opinion pieces; **SL.1.4** describe people, places, things, and events with details/express ideas and feelings clearly

INFORMATIONAL TEXT

Read Together

Garden Good Guys
by Timothy Thomas

Garden Good Guys

by Timothy Thomas

If you have a garden, you should know about bugs. Some bugs are pests that eat the plants. Other bugs eat the pests. They are the garden good guys!

If you want a healthy garden, make sure you have **ladybugs**. Ladybugs eat tiny bugs that snack on garden plants.

You may not think a **praying mantis** is as pretty as a ladybug, but it is a good garden friend. A praying mantis hunts and eats many garden pests.

ladybug

praying mantis

The **big-eyed bug** is tiny. Can you guess how it got its name? Big-eyed bugs eat bugs that harm vegetables.

The **dragonfly** has a long thin body, large eyes, and two sets of wings. Dragonflies are good for gardens and good for you, too. They eat garden pests <u>and</u> mosquitoes!

big-eyed bug

wing

dragonfly

Compare Texts

 Read Together

TEXT TO TEXT

Compare Gardens Think about the gardens in both selections. What helps each garden grow?

TEXT TO SELF

Connect to Experiences Think about how Toad cared for his garden. Write about something you have cared for.

TEXT TO WORLD

Think and Share Tell a partner why people should help plants grow. Take turns speaking. Listen to each other.

 Go Digital

 COMMON CORE

RL.1.1 ask and answer questions about key details; **RL.1.2** retell stories and demonstrate understanding of the message or lesson; **RI.1.2** identify the main topic and retell key details; **W.1.8** recall information from experiences or gather information from sources to answer a question; **SL.1.1a** follow rules for discussions

Grammar

Subject Pronouns Words that can take the place of nouns are called **pronouns**. The pronouns **he**, **she**, and **it** name one. The pronouns **we** and **they** name more than one.

Ben watered the tree. **He** watered the tree.
The tree grew. **It** grew.
Birds loved the tree. **They** loved the tree.
Lily fed the birds. **She** fed the birds.

Choose the correct pronoun to name each picture. Write it on a sheet of paper. Then say a sentence to a partner about each picture. Use the pronoun.

1. she   he

2. they   it

3. it   we

4. they   she

5. we   he

 Grammar in Writing

When you proofread your writing, be sure you have used pronouns correctly.

W.1.3 write narratives; **W.1.5** focus on a topic, respond to questions/suggestions from peers, and add details to strengthen writing; **L.1.1d** use personal, possessive, and indefinite pronouns

Narrative Writing

✓ **Voice** **Dialogue** shows the exact words characters say. Niki wrote about what Frog and Toad did next in the story. Then she added words that told what they said.

Revised Draft

"May I pick some flowers?"

asked Frog. Toad said, "Yes!"

∧ Frog and Toad both wanted

to pick flowers.

Writing Traits Checklist

✓ **Voice** Did I write the exact words characters say?

✓ Did I use time-order words to tell when events happen?

✓ Did I use pronouns correctly?

Look for story events and the exact words Frog and Toad say in Niki's final copy. Then revise your own writing. Use the Checklist.

Final Copy

Picking Flowers

Frog really liked Toad's new garden. "May I pick some flowers?" asked Frog. Toad said, "Yes!" Frog and Toad both wanted to pick flowers. First, they found a nice flower vase. Then they went outside and picked all kinds of flowers. "Frog, you are a good friend. Thank you for helping me grow my flowers," said Toad.

Lesson 22

Amazing Animals

The Ugly Duckling

✓ WORDS TO KNOW
High-Frequency Words

learning

begins

until

eight

young

follow

years

baby

Vocabulary Reader

Context Cards

COMMON CORE

RF.1.3g recognize and read irregularly spelled words

 Go Digital

Words to Know

 Read Together

▶ Read each **Context Card**.

▶ Make up a new sentence that uses a blue word.

1 **learning**

This baby giraffe is learning how to walk.

2 **begins**

The lion cub begins to get stronger.

3 **until**
These owls can't fly until they are older.

4 **eight**
The eight little swans go for a swim.

5 **young**
The young hippo will be very big soon.

6 **follow**
The bear cubs follow their mother.

7 **years**
An elephant can live for seventy years.

8 **baby**
This baby panda is eating plants.

Read and Comprehend

 Go Digital

☑ **TARGET SKILL**

Conclusions Sometimes authors do not tell all the details. Readers must use text evidence from the words and pictures and think about what they already know to make a smart guess about what the author does not tell. This smart guess is a **conclusion.** Use a chart to write details and conclusions about what you read.

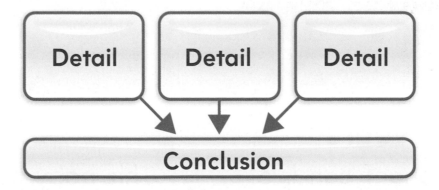

☑ **TARGET STRATEGY**

Visualize As you read, picture in your mind what is happening to help you understand.

RI.1.7 use illustrations and details to describe key ideas

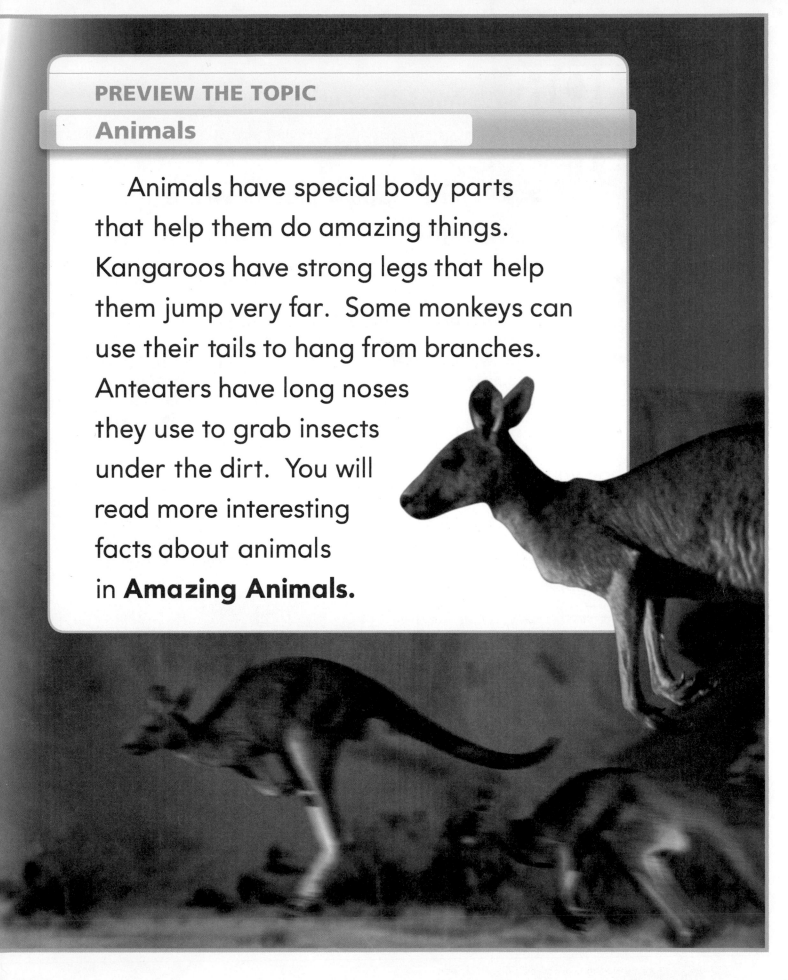

Animals have special body parts that help them do amazing things. Kangaroos have strong legs that help them jump very far. Some monkeys can use their tails to hang from branches. Anteaters have long noses they use to grab insects under the dirt. You will read more interesting facts about animals in **Amazing Animals.**

ANCHOR TEXT

Amazing Animals

✅ TARGET SKILL

Conclusions Use details and what you know to figure out more when you read.

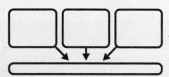

✅ GENRE

Informational text gives facts. As you read, look for:
- information and facts in the words
- photos that show real animals

COMMON CORE **RI.1.4** ask and answer questions to determine or clarify the meaning of words and phrases; **RI.1.7** use illustrations and details to describe key ideas; **RI.1.10** read informational texts

Go Digital

Meet the Author

Gwendolyn Hooks

Gwendolyn Hooks wrote this story because she loves animals. "This story is about wild animals," she explains.
"I don't own any wild animals, but I do have a pet cat."

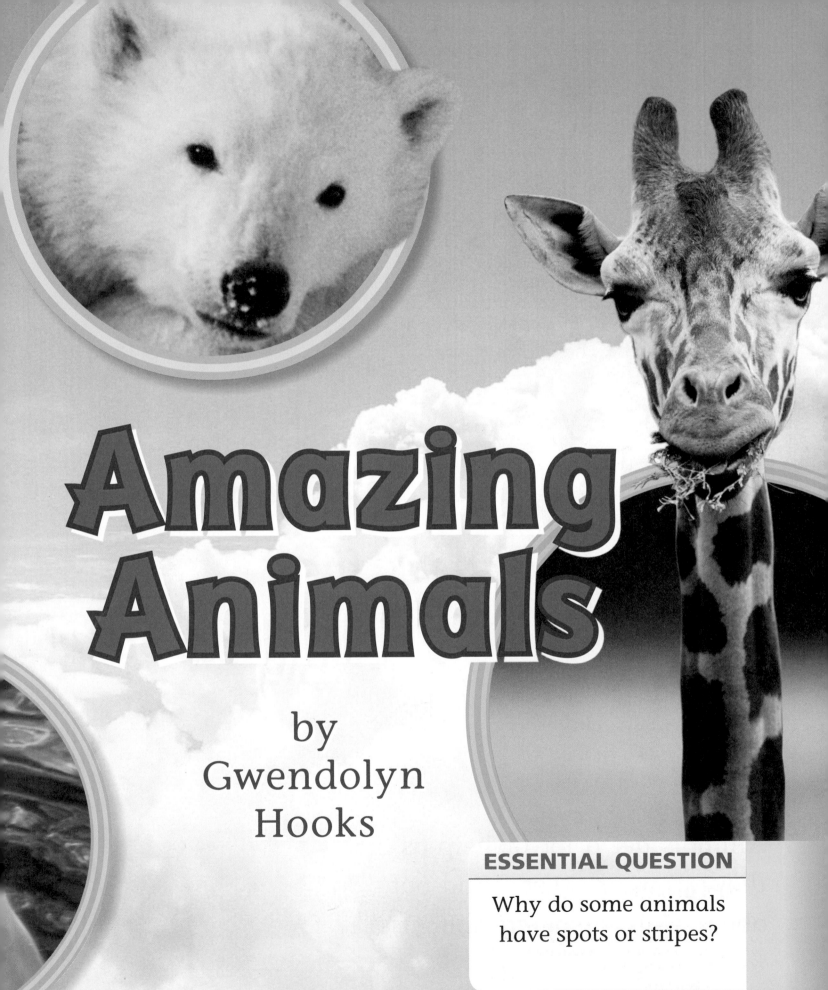

Amazing Animals

by
Gwendolyn
Hooks

ESSENTIAL QUESTION

Why do some animals
have spots or stripes?

Big eyes,

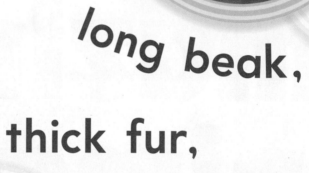

long beak,

thick fur,

big squeak!

Animals get a lot of help as they grow up. Let's find out about **eight** amazing animals.

Polar Bear

A polar bear has thick fur. Each hair is like a tube. The hair has no color, like glass. The sun makes it look white.

How does thick, white fur help?

ANALYZE THE TEXT

Conclusions How do you think the color of their fur helps polar bears?

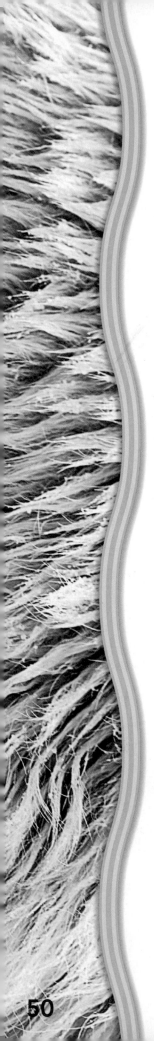

Thick fur helps polar bears stay warm.
The color of their fur looks the same
as snow. This helps them hide.

Where does this cute young polar bear
like to hide?

Elephant

An elephant has a long nose. The nose is called a trunk. It takes many years for an elephant to grow two big teeth. These teeth are called tusks.

How do tusks and a trunk help?

ANALYZE THE TEXT

Using Context What are **tusks**? How do elephants use their tusks?

Elephants use their tusks to scrape bark off trees. Then they eat the bark. These elephants are learning to use their trunks to get water.

Sometimes they will spray water at a friend!

Camel

Some camels have one hump. Some have two. All camels have two rows of eyelashes.

How do humps and thick eyelashes help?

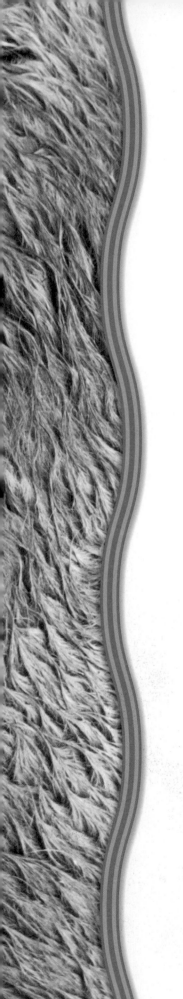

A camel's hump has fat inside. On long trips, a camel's body uses the fat for food. A camel's eyelashes keep out the desert sand.

This baby camel will follow his mother when the herd goes from place to place.

Duck

A duck is a bird. It has two feet, and each foot has three toes. A duck has a beak, too.

How do feet and a beak help?

Ducks use their feet to swim in the water or walk on land. They use their beaks to eat plants and bugs.

Look! This duck uses her beak to clean her friend.

Giraffe

A giraffe has spots. A giraffe has a long neck.

How do spots and a long neck help?

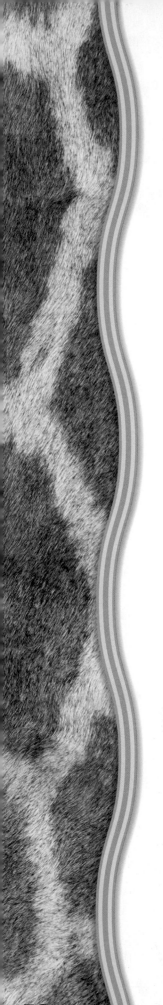

A giraffe's spots help it hide. A giraffe's long neck helps it reach the leaves of trees.

This giraffe's long neck helps her reach her baby. She gives him a big kiss!

Porcupine

A porcupine has soft quills when it is born. The quills get sharp in a day or two.

How do quills help?

Quills help keep a porcupine safe. If an animal begins to come too close, the porcupine backs into it. The sharp quills hurt!

Quills tell this cub to stay away!

Turtle

A turtle has a shell that is very hard.

How does a hard shell help?

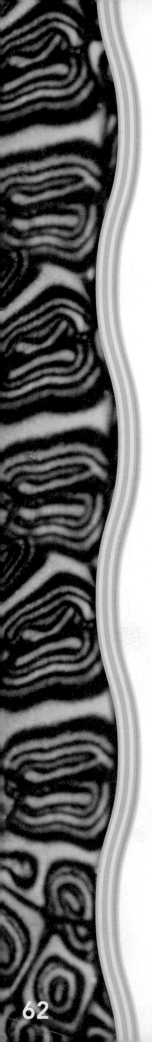

A turtle can hide inside its shell from an animal that may hurt it. The turtle waits until the animal goes away. Then the turtle comes back out.

You're safe now, turtle!

Dolphin

A dolphin's tail has two parts called
flukes. A dolphin has two flippers.

How do tail flukes and flippers help?

A dolphin flips its tail flukes up and down to swim fast. It uses its flippers to turn to the left or right.

These two dolphins swim away fast. Who will be first?

Have fun, dolphins!

Dig Deeper

How to Analyze the Text

Use these pages to learn about Conclusions and Using Context. Then read **Amazing Animals** again.

Conclusions

Use text evidence from **Amazing Animals** to draw **conclusions** about what the author does not say. The author does not tell you what it is like where polar bears live. What do the pictures show? Which words help you? What else do you know about polar bears? Use a chart to write your conclusions.

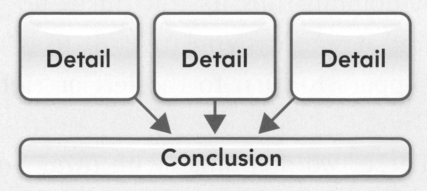

| Detail | Detail | Detail |

Conclusion

 RI.1.4 ask and answer questions to determine or clarify the meaning of words and phrases; **RI.1.7** use illustrations and details to describe key ideas; **L.1.4a** use sentence-level context as a clue to the meaning of a word or phrase

Using Context

An author may use words you do not know. Read the other words in the sentence and look at the picture to help you figure out the word.

What does **trunk** mean in the selection? The words **long nose** and the picture of the elephants are clues that tell you the **trunk** is the long part of an elephant's face. Another good clue is the sentence **The nose is called a trunk.**

 **Read Together**

Your Turn

 **my WriteSmart**

 **Turn and Talk**

Why do some animals have spots or stripes? Talk about how and why some animals in **Amazing Animals** hide. Use text evidence to explain your ideas clearly. Ask questions to understand your partner's ideas.

 Classroom Conversation

Talk about these questions with your class.

1 How do some animals stay safe?

2 How does a dolphin's tail help it live?

3 Tell about some parts other animals have that help them. How do your hands help you?

Response Which is the most amazing animal in **Amazing Animals**? Draw a picture of it and label its body parts. Use text evidence to write reasons why the animal is amazing. Tell how special body parts help that animal.

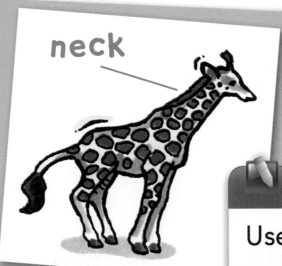

neck

Writing Tip

Use words like **because** or **so** to show how your opinion and reasons go together.

 COMMON CORE **RI.1.7** use illustrations and details to describe key ideas; **W.1.1** write opinion pieces; **W.1.5** focus on a topic, respond to questions/suggestions from peers, and add details to strengthen writing; **SL.1.3** ask and answer questions about what a speaker says; **SL.1.4** describe people, places, things, and events with details/express ideas and feelings clearly

FOLKTALE

Read Together

The Ugly Duckling

☑ GENRE

A **folktale** is an old story that has been told for many years. Sometimes it teaches a lesson.

☑ TEXT FOCUS

Many tales have **storytelling phrases**. Sometimes stories begin with **once upon a time**. Sometimes they end with **happily ever after**. What do these words mean in this story?

COMMON CORE **RL.1.4** identify words and phrases that suggest feelings or appeal to senses; **RL.1.10** read prose and poetry

The Ugly Duckling

Once upon a time, a duck sat on eight eggs. One day, all but one of the eggs hatched. The ducks waited until the last baby bird came out. He was big and gray. The other ducks thought he was ugly.

Each day the ducklings would follow
Mother Duck. They were learning to be
ducks. The other ducks did not want to
play with the ugly duckling. He felt sad.
One day he left.

Winter soon came. A farmer found the
ugly duckling. "I must take you home
before it begins to snow," he said.

When spring came, the farmer took the duckling to a pond. The duckling saw himself in the water. He felt like many years had passed. He had changed!

Now he knew he was not an ugly duckling. He was a young swan. He and the other swans lived happily ever after.

Compare Texts

Read Together

TEXT TO TEXT

Compare Selections Which selection is true? Which is make-believe? Tell a small group how you know. Use text evidence to help you explain.

TEXT TO SELF

Think About Characters How does the duckling in **The Ugly Duckling** change in the story? Tell how you have changed since you were a baby.

TEXT TO WORLD

Connect to Science Pick an animal. How does it grow? Use books and other sources to find out.

COMMON CORE **RL.1.3** describe characters, settings, and major events; **RL.1.5** explain major differences between story books and informational books; **RL.1.9** compare and contrast adventures and experiences of characters; **RI.1.7** use illustrations and details to describe key ideas; **W.1.8** recall information from experiences or gather information from sources to answer a question

Grammar

The Pronouns I and Me Use **I** in the subject of a sentence and **me** in the predicate. Name yourself last when you talk about yourself and others.

Correct

Sara and **I** like baby animals.

Not Correct

I and Sara like baby animals.
Me and Sara like baby animals.

Correct

The puppy licks **Jill and me.**

Not Correct

The puppy licks **me and Jill.**
The puppy licks **Jill and I.**

 **Try This!**

Write the correct words to finish each
sentence. Use another sheet of paper.
Read your sentences to a partner.

1. _____?_____ saw a piglet.
   Dad and I   I and Dad

2. The chicks looked at _____?_____.
   Jake and me   me and Jake

3. _____?_____ fed one kitten.
   I and Ana   Ana and I

4. The cubs ran from _____?_____.
   Liz and I   Liz and me

 Grammar in Writing

When you proofread your writing, be sure
to use the pronouns **I** and **me** correctly.
Remember to capitalize **I**.

W.1.3 write narratives; **W.1.5** focus on a topic, respond to questions/suggestions from peers, and add details to strengthen writing; **L.1.1e** use verbs to convey sense of past, present, and future

Narrative Writing

✔ **Word Choice** Good **story sentences** have exact verbs that help readers picture what the story characters are doing.

Troy wrote about a baby bird. Later, he changed **went** to a more exact verb.

Revised Draft

Then Jay ~~went~~ into the air.

        flew
              ^

Writing Traits Checklist

✔ **Word Choice** Do my sentences have exact verbs?

✔ Did I tell what happened in order?

✔ Do I need to delete any words?

✔ Does my last sentence tell the ending?

Look for story events and exact verbs in Troy's final copy. Then revise your writing. Use the Checklist.

Final Copy

Flying Lesson

Jay stood quietly by the nest.

First, he watched his mom.

Then Jay flew into the air.

He sailed high above the garden.

Jay soared all the way home.

EZRA JACK KEATS
WHISTLE FOR WILLIE

Pet Poems

☑ **WORDS TO KNOW**
High-Frequency Words

house
along
together
boy
father
again
nothing
began

Vocabulary Reader

Context Cards

COMMON CORE
RF.1.3g recognize and read irregularly spelled words

Go Digital

Words to Know

Read Together

▶ Read each **Context Card**.

▶ Ask a question that uses one of the blue words.

1 **house**

They learned how to build a house for birds.

2 **along**

He rode carefully along the bike path.

3 together

The baby can clap her hands **together** now.

4 boy

The **boy** teaches his sister to read.

5 father

My **father** teaches me how to swim.

6 again

We went out on the ice **again** to practice.

7 nothing

At first **nothing** fit, but he finished the puzzle.

8 began

She **began** to take violin lessons.

WHISTLE FOR WILLIE

Read and Comprehend

Read Together

Go Digital

☑ **TARGET SKILL**

Cause and Effect Sometimes one story event causes another event to happen. The **cause** happens first. The **effect** is what happens next. As you read, ask yourself what happens and why. You can use a chart to help you understand events.

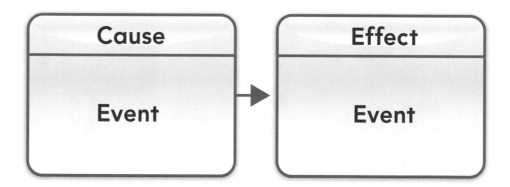

Cause		Effect
Event	→	Event

☑ **TARGET STRATEGY**

Monitor/Clarify If a part doesn't make sense, you can ask questions, reread, and use the pictures for help.

COMMON CORE **RL.1.1** ask and answer questions about key details; **RL.1.3** describe characters, settings, and major events; **RL.1.7** use illustrations and details to describe characters, setting, or events

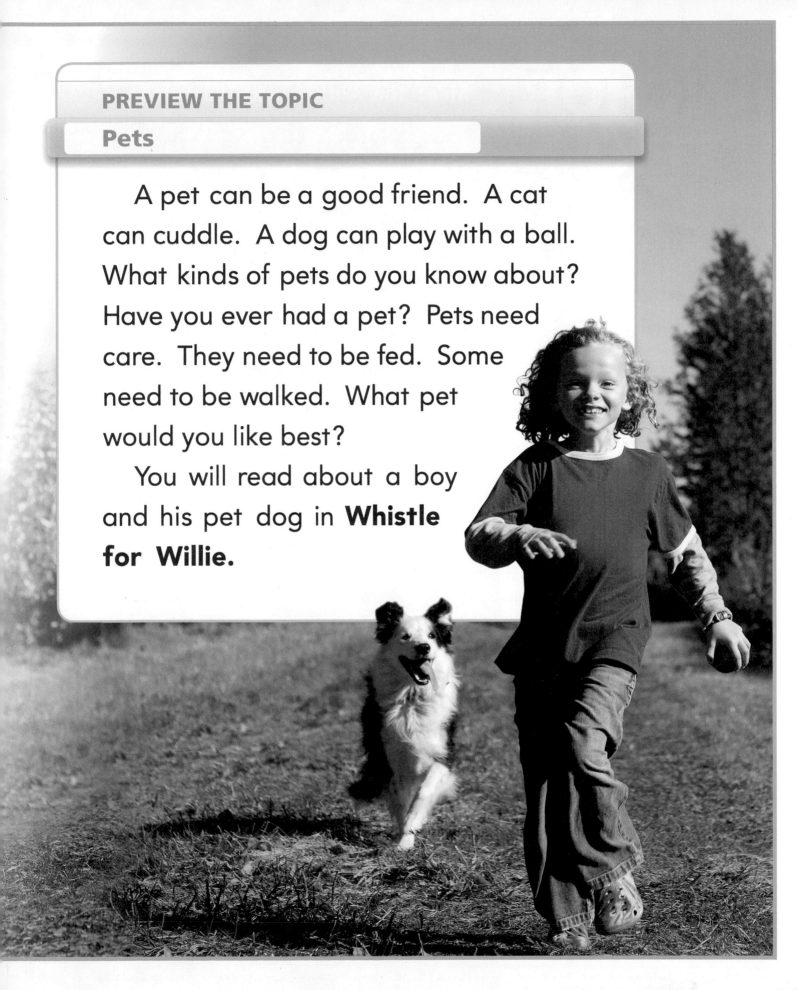

A pet can be a good friend. A cat can cuddle. A dog can play with a ball. What kinds of pets do you know about? Have you ever had a pet? Pets need care. They need to be fed. Some need to be walked. What pet would you like best?

You will read about a boy and his pet dog in **Whistle for Willie.**

ANCHOR TEXT

☑ TARGET SKILL

Cause and Effect
Tell what happens and why.

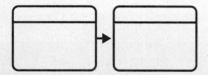

☑ GENRE

Realistic fiction is a story that could happen in real life. As you read, look for:

▸ events that could really happen
▸ characters who do things real people and animals do

COMMON CORE **RL.1.3** describe characters, settings, and major events; **RL.1.4** identify words and phrases that suggest feelings or appeal to senses; **RL.1.10** read prose and poetry

Meet the Author and Illustrator

Ezra Jack Keats

Ezra Jack Keats wrote and illustrated books for children. When Mr. Keats was a boy, he drew pictures on the kitchen table. His mother was so proud, she kept the art rather than wash the table.

WHISTLE FOR WILLIE

by Ezra Jack Keats

ESSENTIAL QUESTION

How can you take good care of a pet?

Oh, how Peter wished he could whistle!

He saw a boy playing with his dog. Whenever the boy whistled, the dog ran straight to him.

ANALYZE THE TEXT

Cause and Effect What happens when the boy whistles?

85

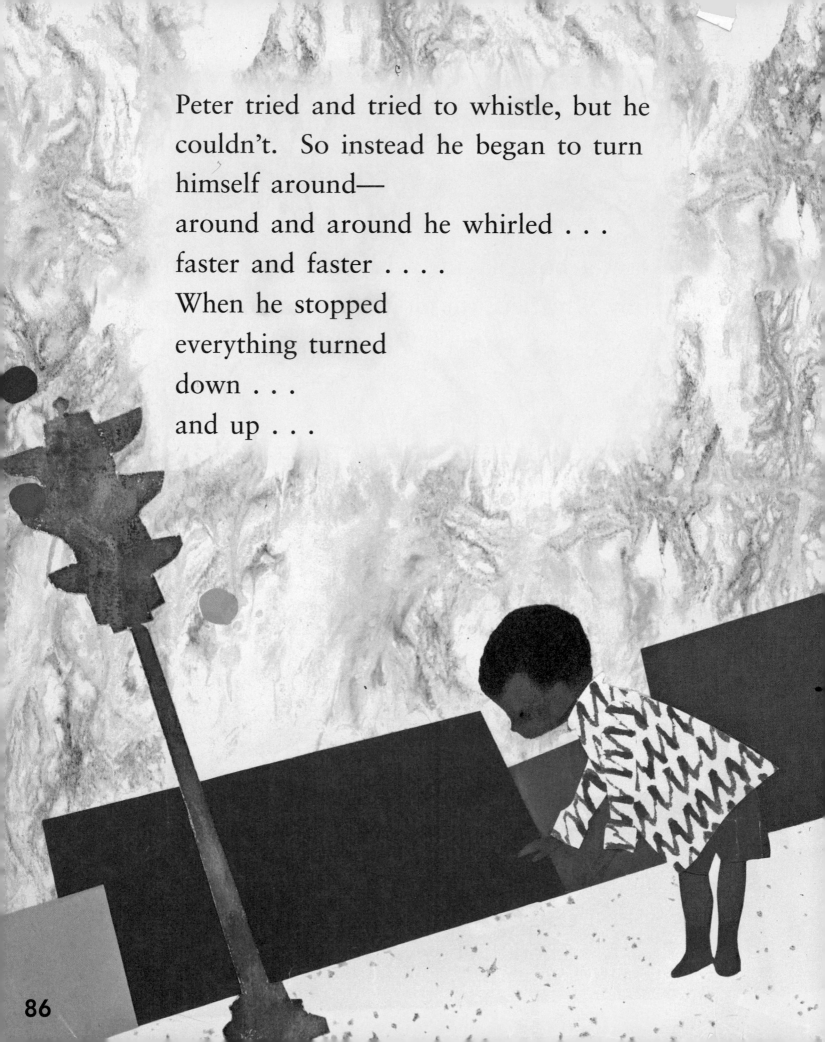

Peter tried and tried to whistle, but he
couldn't. So instead he began to turn
himself around—
around and around he whirled . . .
faster and faster . . . .
When he stopped
everything turned
down . . .
and up . . .

and up . . .
and down . . .
and around
and around.

Peter saw his dog, Willie, coming. Quick as a wink, he hid in an empty carton lying on the sidewalk.

ANALYZE THE TEXT

Figurative Language What does **quick as a wink** mean? Why do you think so?

"Wouldn't it be funny if I whistled?" Peter thought. "Willie would stop and look all around to see who it was."

Peter tried again to whistle—but still he couldn't. So Willie just walked on.

Peter got out of the carton and started home.
On the way he took some colored chalks out
of his pocket and drew a long, long line
right up to his door.

He stood there and tried to whistle
again. He blew till his cheeks were
tired. But nothing happened.

He went into his house and put on his father's old hat to make himself feel more grown-up. He looked into the mirror to practice whistling. Still no whistle!

When his mother saw what he was doing,
Peter pretended that he was his father.
He said, "I've come home early today, dear.
Is Peter here?"
His mother answered, "Why no, he's outside
with Willie."
"Well, I'll go out and look for them," said Peter.

First he walked along a crack in the sidewalk. Then he tried to run away from his shadow.

He jumped off his shadow. But when he landed they were together again.

He came to the corner
where the carton was,
and who should he see
but Willie!

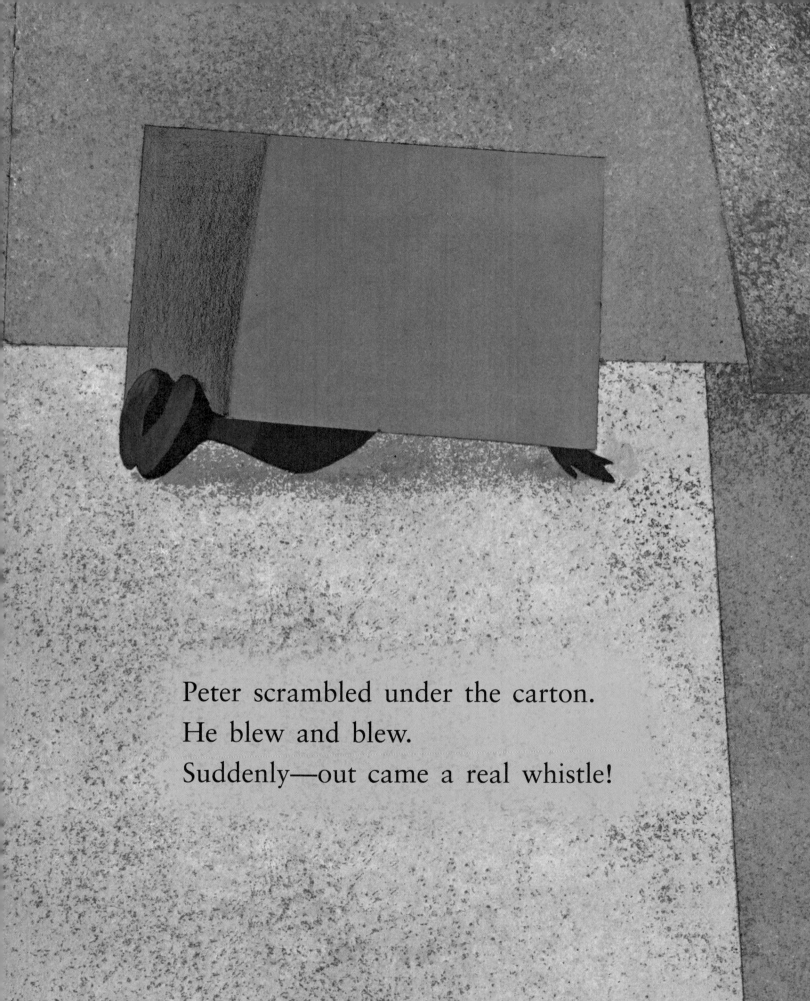

Peter scrambled under the carton.
He blew and blew.
Suddenly—out came a real whistle!

Willie stopped and looked around to
see who it was.

"It's me," Peter shouted, and stood up.
Willie raced straight to him.

Peter ran home to show his father and
mother what he could do.
They loved Peter's whistling. So did Willie.

Peter's mother asked him and Willie
to go on an errand to the grocery store.
He whistled all the way there,
and he whistled all the way home.

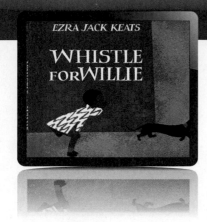

Dig Deeper

Read Together

How to Analyze the Text

Use these pages to learn about Cause and Effect and Figurative Language. Then read **Whistle for Willie** again.

Cause and Effect

In **Whistle for Willie**, story events cause other events to happen. The **cause** is the reason why something else happens. The **effect** is what happens next. In the story, Peter keeps trying to whistle. This is the cause. What happens because he tries to whistle? Use a chart like this to show why important events happen.

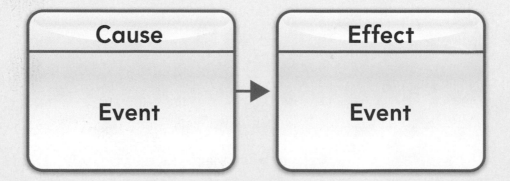

Cause		Effect
Event	→	Event

COMMON CORE **RL.1.3** describe characters, settings, and major events; **RL.1.4** identify words and phrases that suggest feelings or appeal to senses; **L.1.6** use words and phrases acquired through conversations, reading and being read to, and responding to texts

Go Digital

Figurative Language

Authors often use words in interesting ways to help you picture what is happening. The story says that Peter **scrambled under** the carton when he sees Willie. These words help you know how Peter moves. He does not go under the carton slowly. He goes under very quickly. What other words does the author use in interesting ways?

Your Turn

RETURN TO THE ESSENTIAL QUESTION

 Turn and Talk

How can you take good care of a pet? How does Peter take care of Willie? Use text evidence to help you explain. Talk about what you know about taking care of a pet. Tell your ideas clearly.

Classroom Conversation

Talk about these questions with your class.

1 What lesson can you learn from Peter?

2 Why does Peter want to learn to whistle?

3 Peter learns how to whistle. What have you learned how to do because you kept trying?

Response What would Willie say if he could talk? What would he say happened? Write sentences that tell the story the way Willie would tell it.

Writing Tip

Use words like **first, next, then,** and **finally** to tell when things happen.

COMMON CORE **RL.1.1** ask and answer questions about key details; **RL.1.2** retell stories and demonstrate understanding of the message or lesson; **RL.1.3** describe characters, settings, and major events; **W.1.3** write narratives; **SL.1.4** describe people, places, things, and events with details/express ideas and feelings clearly

POETRY

Read Together

Pet Poems

Poetry uses words to describe pictures and feelings. Listen for interesting words in each poem. Clap along with the rhythm, or beat.

✓ **TEXT FOCUS**

Words **rhyme** if they have the same ending sound. Which poems use words that rhyme?

COMMON CORE **RL.1.10** read prose and poetry; **L.1.6** use words and phrases acquired through conversations, reading and being read to, and responding to texts

Pet Poems

This poem began as a folk song. Read it along with your class. Then sing it together.

Bingo

There was a farmer had a dog,
And Bingo was his name, O!
B – I – N – G – O,
B – I – N – G – O,
B – I – N – G – O,
And Bingo was his name, O!

Can someone in your class read this poem in Spanish? Now read it again in English.

Caballito blanco, reblanco

Caballito blanco,
reblanco,
sácame de aquí,
llévame hasta el puerto
donde yo nací.

Little White Horse

Little horse
White as snow
Take me where
I long to go.
Take me to the port
By the sea
Where I was born
And long to be.

traditional folk poem

What kind of pet would you like to have? Would you like a furry pet or a pet with scales?

PET SNAKE

No trace of fuzz.
No bit of fur.
No growling bark,
or gentle purr.
No cozy cuddle.
No sloppy kiss.
All he really does
is hisssssssssss.

by Rebecca Kai Dotlich

Write About a Pet

Write a poem about a pet. Use words with the same beginning sounds. Use some rhyming words, too.

Compare Texts

Read
Together

TEXT TO TEXT

Compare Pets How is Willie different from the pet snake in the poem? Write words that tell what Willie looks like and what he can do. Draw a picture.

TEXT TO SELF

Describe a Pet Find words in the poems that tell what the pets look like. Use some of these words and your own words to describe a pet you like.

TEXT TO WORLD

Research Pets Work with classmates. Use books and other sources to find out how to take care of a pet. Write steps.

Go
Digital

COMMON
CORE
RL.1.3 describe characters, settings, and major events; **RL.1.4** identify words and phrases that suggest feelings or appeal to senses; **RL.1.9** compare and contrast adventures and experiences of characters; **W.1.7** participate in shared research and writing projects; **SL.1.4** describe people, places, things, and events with details/express ideas and feelings clearly

Grammar

Possessive Pronouns Some **pronouns** show that something belongs to someone. This kind of pronoun can come before a noun or at the end of a sentence.

This is **my** dog.
This dog is **mine**.

I am using **your** chalk.
The chalk is **yours**.

That is **his** shadow.
That shadow is **his**.

I am wearing **her** hat.
This hat is **hers**.

Write the correct pronoun
to finish each sentence.
Use another sheet of paper.

1. I have a dog. Little Cleo is _____**?**_.
   mine   mines

2. This is her dish. The dish is _____**?**_.
   his   hers

3. I whistle. Cleo hears ____**?**____ whistle.
   my   mine

4. She follows me to ____**?**____ house.
   your   yours

5. Cleo thinks your toys are ____**?**____!
   her   hers

 Grammar in Writing

When you proofread your writing, be sure
you have used pronouns correctly.

W.1.3 write narratives; **W.1.5** focus on a topic, respond to questions/suggestions from peers, and add details to strengthen writing; **L.1.1d** use personal, possessive, and indefinite pronouns

Narrative Writing

✔ **Organization** When you write sentences for a **story summary**, tell the important events in the order they happened.

Abby wrote a summary of **Whistle for Willie**. Later, she moved one sentence.

Read Together

my WriteSmart

Go Digital

Revised Draft

Peter kept trying to whistle.

He practiced in a mirror.

~~He went into his house.~~

Writing Traits Checklist

✔ **Organization** Did I tell the events in order?

✔ Do I need to add more important details?

✔ Did I use the correct pronouns?

114

Look for events in the correct order in Abby's final copy. Then revise your own writing. Use the Checklist.

Final Copy

Whistle for Willie

Peter kept trying to whistle.
Then he went into his house.
He practiced in a mirror.
When Peter's mom saw him,
he pretended to be his dad.
Then Peter went outside.
He saw Willie, so he hid
under the carton.
Finally, Peter whistled and
Willie ran to him.
Peter was so happy!

☑ **WORDS TO KNOW**
High-Frequency Words

ready
country
soil
kinds
earth
almost
covers
warms

Vocabulary Reader

Context Cards

COMMON CORE RF.1.3g recognize and read irregularly spelled words

 Go Digital

Words to Know

 Read Together

▶ Read each **Context Card**.

▶ Describe a picture, using the blue word.

1 **ready**

We are ready to pick apples.

2 **country**

We live in the country.

3 soil

We planted the flowers in the soil.

4 kinds

There are many kinds of butterflies here.

5 earth

She covers the seeds with earth.

6 almost

The apples are almost ripe.

7 covers

Pollen covers the bee.

8 warms

The oven warms our apple pie!

Read and Comprehend

✓ **TARGET SKILL**

Sequence of Events Many selections tell about things in the order in which they happen. This order is called the **sequence of events**. Think about what happens first, next, and last as you read. You can use a flow chart to keep track of the sequence of events.

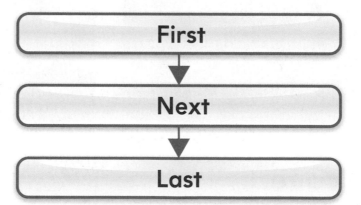

First

↓

Next

↓

Last

✓ **TARGET STRATEGY**

Question Ask yourself questions as you read. Look for text evidence in the selection to answer your questions.

COMMON CORE

RI.1.1 ask and answer questions about key details; **RI.1.3** describe the connection between individuals, events, ideas, or information in a text

118

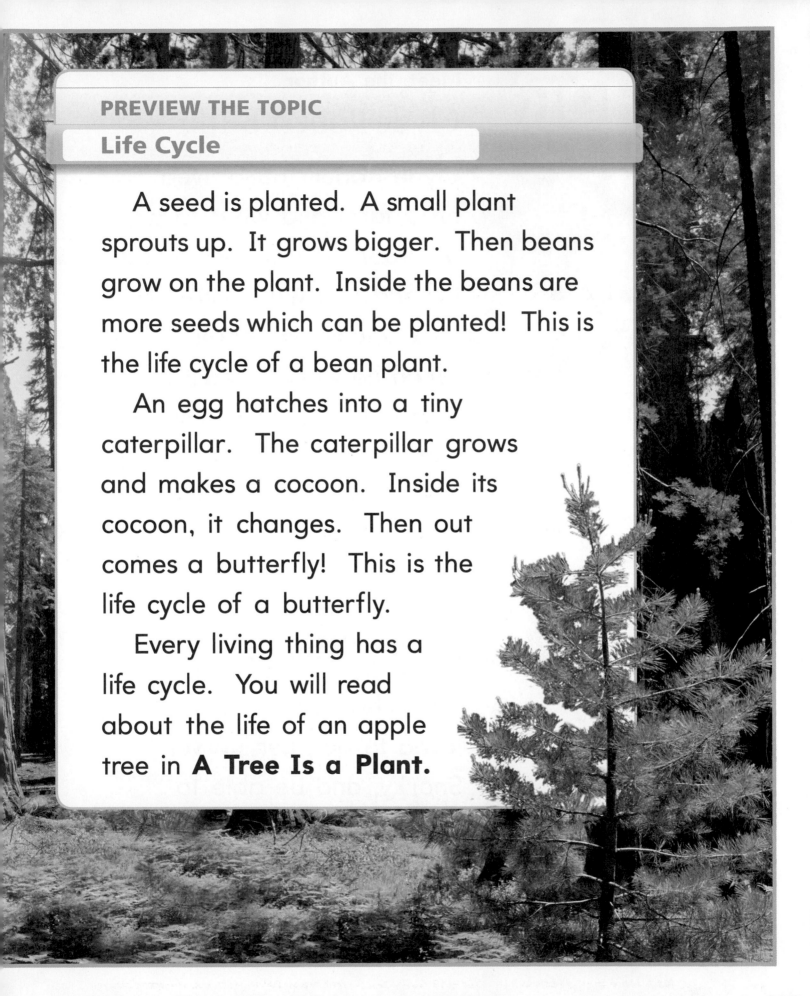

A seed is planted. A small plant sprouts up. It grows bigger. Then beans grow on the plant. Inside the beans are more seeds which can be planted! This is the life cycle of a bean plant.

An egg hatches into a tiny caterpillar. The caterpillar grows and makes a cocoon. Inside its cocoon, it changes. Then out comes a butterfly! This is the life cycle of a butterfly.

Every living thing has a life cycle. You will read about the life of an apple tree in **A Tree Is a Plant.**

ANCHOR TEXT

A Tree Is a PLANT

by Clyde Robert Bulla
Illustrated by Stacey Schuett

☑ **TARGET SKILL**

Sequence of Events
Tell the order in which events happen.

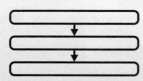

☑ **GENRE**

Informational text gives facts. As you read, look for:

▸ information and facts in the words
▸ pictures that show details about the real world

COMMON CORE **RI.1.3** describe the connection between individuals, events, ideas, or information in a text; **RI.1.4** ask and answer questions to determine or clarify the meaning of words and phrases; **RI.1.10** read informational texts

Go Digital

Meet the Author

Clyde Robert Bulla

Clyde Robert Bulla lived on a farm and went to a one-room school. He loved to read and write, but he also had to do chores. When he was 10 years old, Clyde entered an essay contest and won a prize! When he grew up, he wrote many books for children.

Meet the Illustrator

Stacey Schuett

As a child, Stacey Schuett loved to ride her horse, Snorky, and be able to observe nature. She puts a lot of what she remembers in her drawings and paintings.

A Tree Is a Plant

by Clyde Robert Bulla

illustrated by Stacey Schuett

CONIFER

MAPLE

PALMS

PERSIMMON

WILLOW

LEMON

A tree is a plant.

A tree is the biggest plant that grows.

Most kinds of trees grow from seeds
the way most small plants do.

There are many kinds of trees.

Here are a few of them.

How many do you know?

This tree grows in the country.
It might grow in your yard, too.
Do you know what kind it is?
This is an apple tree.

This apple tree came from a seed.

The seed was small.

It grew inside an apple.

Have you ever seen an apple seed?

Ask an adult to help you cut
an apple in two.

The seeds are in the center.

They look like this.

Most apple trees come from seeds
that are planted.
Sometimes an apple tree grows
from a seed that falls
to the ground.

The wind blows leaves over the seed.
The wind blows soil over the seed.

All winter the seed lies
under the leaves and the soil.
All winter the seed lies under
the ice and snow and is
pushed into the ground.

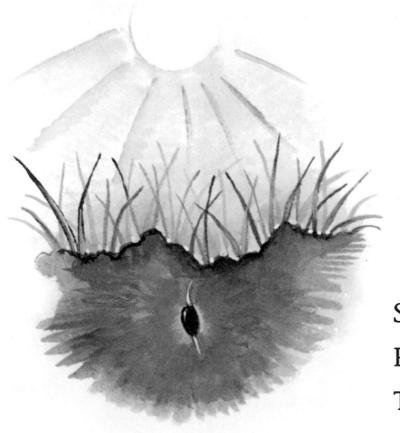

Spring comes.
Rain falls.
The sun comes out
and warms the earth.
The seed begins to grow.

At first the young plant does not
look like a tree.
The tree is very small.
It is only a stem with two leaves.
It has no apples on it.
A tree must grow up before it
has apples on it.
Each year the tree grows.
It grows tall.
In seven years it is so tall that
you can stand under its branches.
In the spring there are
blossoms on the tree.
Spring is apple-blossom time.

ANALYZE THE TEXT

Sequence of Events After many years, what happens to the little plant?

The blossoms last only a few days.

Then they fall to the ground.

Now there are green leaves on the tree.

Among the leaves there are small apples.
The apples are where the blossoms were
before. The apples are green, and they
are almost too small for you to see.
The apples grow slowly.
They grow all during the spring and
the summer.

In the fall they are large and ripe.
They are ready to eat.
We can see the apples and the leaves
on the branches.
We can see the branches growing
out of the trunk.
We can see the trunk
growing out of
the ground.

We can see the bark of the tree.
The bark covers the branches and
the trunk like a coat.
But there is a part of the tree
that we cannot see.

ANALYZE THE TEXT

Figurative Language Why
do you think the author says
the bark is like a coat?

We cannot see the roots.

They are under the ground.

Some of the roots are large.

Some of them are as small as hairs.

The roots grow like branches under the ground.

A tree could not live without roots.

Roots hold the trunk in the ground.
Roots keep the tree from falling when
the wind blows.
Roots keep the rain from washing
the tree out of the ground.

Roots do something more.

They take water from the ground.

They carry the water into the trunk of the tree.

The trunk carries the water to the branches.

The branches carry the water to the leaves.

Hundreds and hundreds of leaves
grow on the branches.

The leaves make food from water and air.

They make food when the sun shines.

The food goes into the branches.

It goes into the trunk and roots.

It goes to every part
of the tree.

137

Fall comes and winter is near.

The work of the leaves is over.

The leaves turn yellow and brown.

The leaves die and fall to the ground.

Now the tree is bare.

All winter it looks dead.

But the tree is not dead.

Under its coat of bark, the tree is alive.

Spring comes again. Rain falls.

The sun warms the earth.
The tree blossoms, and new leaves grow.
As long as it lives, the apple tree grows.
As long as it lives, the apple tree blossoms
in the spring, and apples grow on it.

When do you like apple trees best?

In spring when they are covered with blossoms?

In summer when they are covered with leaves?

In winter when they are bare?

Or in fall when they are covered with apples?

Dig Deeper

Read Together

How to Analyze the Text

Use these pages to learn about Sequence of Events and Figurative Language. Then read **A Tree Is a Plant** again.

Sequence of Events

The order in which events happen is the **sequence of events.** **A Tree Is a Plant** tells about the events in the life of a tree. The apple tree begins as a seed. What happens next? When the tree is big, what happens to it in the spring, summer, fall, and winter? Use a flow chart to show the order of important events.

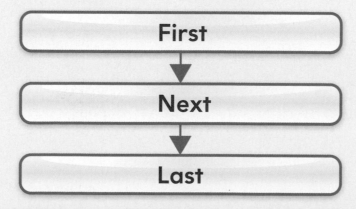

First

↓

Next

↓

Last

COMMON CORE

RI.1.3 describe the connection between individuals, events, ideas, or information in a text; **RI.1.4** ask and answer questions to determine or clarify the meaning of words and phrases; **L.1.6** use words and phrases acquired through conversations, reading and being read to, and responding to texts

  Go Digital

Figurative Language

Authors sometimes tell how two things are the same by using the word **like** or **as**. This word choice is called a **simile.**

In **A Tree Is a Plant,** the author says that the roots are **as small as hairs**. Do you think this means the roots are thick or thin? Describe how you picture the roots. What else does the author say the roots are like?

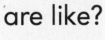

Your Turn

 my WriteSmart

RETURN TO THE ESSENTIAL QUESTION

 **Turn and Talk**

What happens to a tree as it grows? Talk about the order of events in **A Tree Is a Plant.** Could the author have used a different order? Why or why not? Use text evidence from the selection in your answers.

 Classroom Conversation

Talk about these questions with your class.

1 Why are a tree's roots important?

2 How do leaves help a tree?

3 What is the order of the seasons? How does the apple tree change during the seasons?

Response Make a chart that shows the steps in an apple tree's life. Draw what the tree looks like at each step. Label the parts of the tree.

Then write a fact you learned about how apple trees grow. Use text evidence, such as words and pictures in the selection, for ideas.

leaves

branch

bark

trunk

Writing Tip

Add labels to give more information about pictures.

COMMON CORE

RI.1.3 describe the connection between individuals, events, ideas, or information in a text; **RI.1.7** use illustrations and details to describe key ideas; **W.1.8** recall information from experiences or gather information from sources to answer a question; **SL.1.4** describe people, places, things, and events with details/express ideas and feelings clearly

INFORMATIONAL TEXT

Grow, **Apples,** Grow!

Read Together

☑ GENRE

Informational text gives facts about a topic. It can be a textbook, article, or website. What facts can you learn from this selection about apples?

☑ TEXT FOCUS

Captions are sentences that tell more about a picture or photograph. What information can you learn from the captions in this selection?

COMMON CORE **RI.1.5** know and use text features to locate facts or information; **RI.1.10** read informational texts

 Go Digital

Grow, Apples, Grow!

Every apple tree starts with a tiny apple seed. An apple tree grows roots, which take in water and food from the soil. The apple tree also grows leaves, which make food from sunlight.

apple

seed

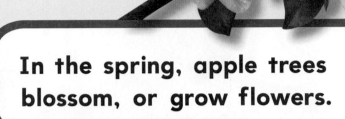

In the spring, apple trees blossom, or grow flowers.

The flowers drop off, and apples grow in their place.

In the fall, the apples are ready to be picked.

People make many kinds of foods from apples.

Apples may be sweet, or tart, or soft, or crisp, or crunchy. But one thing apples always are is

munchy,

munchy,

munchy!

Compare Texts

Read Together

TEXT TO TEXT

Compare Both selections are about apple trees. How are the pictures alike and different? Make a chart. Write text evidence from each selection about apple trees during one season.

Spring

A Tree Is a Plant	Grow, Apples, Grow!

TEXT TO SELF

Write a Story Pretend that your class hiked to an apple tree and back. Write a story. Tell what happened in order.

TEXT TO WORLD

Look It Up Find out more about trees. Write the most interesting fact you learn. Draw a picture of it.

COMMON CORE **RI.1.1** ask and answer questions about key details; **RI.1.7** use illustrations and details to describe key ideas; **RI.1.9** identify similarities in and differences between texts on the same topic; **W.1.3** write narratives; **W.1.7** participate in shared research and writing projects

Grammar

Indefinite Pronouns There are special **pronouns** that stand for the names of people or things. They do not take the place of a noun for a certain person or thing, though.

Anyone can pick apples.
I want to learn **everything** about apples.
Someone planted the apple seeds long ago.
Who has **something** to put the apples in?
Everyone at home loves apples!

Try This!

Use a pronoun from the box to complete each sentence. There may be more than one right answer. Write each sentence on a sheet of paper. Take turns reading your sentences with a partner.

anyone	**something**	**someone**
everything	**everyone**	

1. We saw _____ picking an apple.

2. _____ can eat apples.

3. I like _____ about apples.

4. _____ rides to the apple farm.

 Grammar in Writing

When you proofread your writing, make sure your indefinite pronouns make sense where they are used.

Reading-Writing Workshop: **Prewrite**

Narrative Writing

✓ **Ideas**   When you plan a **story,** think of your characters. How do they look? What do they like? What problem do they have?

Deval drew pictures of his characters. Then he wrote clear details about them.

Exploring a Topic

fly fast   friends

like apples

Prewriting Checklist

✓ Did I write details to describe my characters?

✓ Did I plan a problem my characters will solve?

✓ Does my story have a beginning, a middle, and an ending?

Look in Deval's Story Map for a problem his characters will solve. Now make a Story Map for your own story. Use the Checklist.

Story Map

Characters	**Setting**
2 bees named Burt and Al	a beehive

Plot

Beginning

bees are best friends

fly fast

like apples

Middle

Al moves (problem!)

bees talk on the phone

Ending

Burt brings apples to Al

Lesson 25

The New Friend
by Maria Puncel · Illustrations by Ed Martinez

Symbols of Our Country

☑ WORDS TO KNOW
High-Frequency Words

city
myself
school
party
seven
buy
please
family

Vocabulary Reader

Moving

Context Cards

COMMON CORE

RF.1.3g recognize and read irregularly spelled words

Go Digital

Words to Know

Read Together

▶ Read each **Context Card**.

▶ Use a blue word to tell about something you did.

---

1 **city**

They moved to the city from the country.

---

2 **myself**

I took the box into the house all by myself.

3 **school**

He met many new friends at school.

4 **party**

They had a party for their new classmate.

5 **seven**

She will bring seven apples to school.

6 **buy**

She will buy a plant for her friend.

7 **please**

"Please play with us," they said.

8 **family**

They invited the family to come in.

Read and Comprehend

Read Together

Go Digital

☑ **TARGET SKILL**

Understanding Characters Remember that you can learn a lot about what story **characters** are like from their words and actions. Use what the characters say and do as clues. Figure out how they feel and why they act the way they do. You can list the clues, or text evidence, on a chart.

Words	Actions	Feelings

☑ **TARGET STRATEGY**

Summarize Stop to tell about the important events as you read.

RL.1.3 describe characters, settings, and major events; **RL.1.7** use illustrations and details to describe characters, setting, or events

COMMON CORE

162

Learning About Our Country

We live in the United States of America. People have come to this country from all over the world. You learn about our country at school. You can read books about our country, too. What do you know about our country?

You will read about a boy who moves to the United States in **The New Friend**.

ANCHOR TEXT

The New Friend
by María Puncel · Illustrations by Ed Martinez

✓ TARGET SKILL

Understanding Characters Tell about characters' words, actions, and feelings.

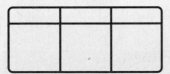

✓ GENRE

Realistic fiction is a story that could happen in real life. As you read, look for:

▶ characters who act like real people
▶ events that could really happen

COMMON CORE **RL.1.3** describe characters, settings, and major events; **RL.1.6** identify who is telling the story; **RL.1.10** read prose and poetry

Meet the Author

María Puncel

María Puncel lives in Spain. She writes her books in Spanish. Many of them have been translated into English, including **El Amigo Nuevo**.

Meet the Illustrator

Ed Martinez

Ed Martinez grew up with a painter in the family. His father was an artist! As a boy, Mr. Martinez got started by drawing horses. Now he draws pictures for magazines and books.

The New Friend

by María Puncel • illustrations by Ed Martinez

ESSENTIAL QUESTION

What can you learn
from someone who is
from another country?

Martin, Luis, and I lived in the city. Next door was an old house. No one had lived there for a long time.

ANALYZE THE TEXT

Narrator Who is the narrator? Why do you think so?

One day a work crew came with pails and brushes. They started to wash and paint the empty house.

After they were done, and the paint had dried, the house looked pretty and new.

The next day a big truck pulled up. It was full of crates and boxes. A crew unloaded the boxes off the truck. A new family would soon live there.

Today Luis went over to the house next door.
He met a boy called Makoto. Then we all met
Makoto. Makoto was seven years old—just
like us.

Before long, we found out that Makoto played soccer. He could keep running and running. He was good at learning things, too. He learned all of our names by the end of the game.

Soon Makoto's family was all moved in. We met his mother and father. They were glad that Makoto had made some new friends.

While Makoto's mother and father went to buy food, Makoto stayed and played with us.

When Makoto's mother and father rejoined us, Martin, Makoto, and I helped them carry the bags into the house.

Makoto said he would show us around his house. Then we went up to look at Makoto's room.

Makoto still had a lot of boxes to unpack. He had some nice toys and kites. He said that on the next windy day, we could bring his kites outside and fly them. He said I could fly a kite by myself.

Then we went outside to look
at Makoto's pictures from Japan.
He had them in a green book.

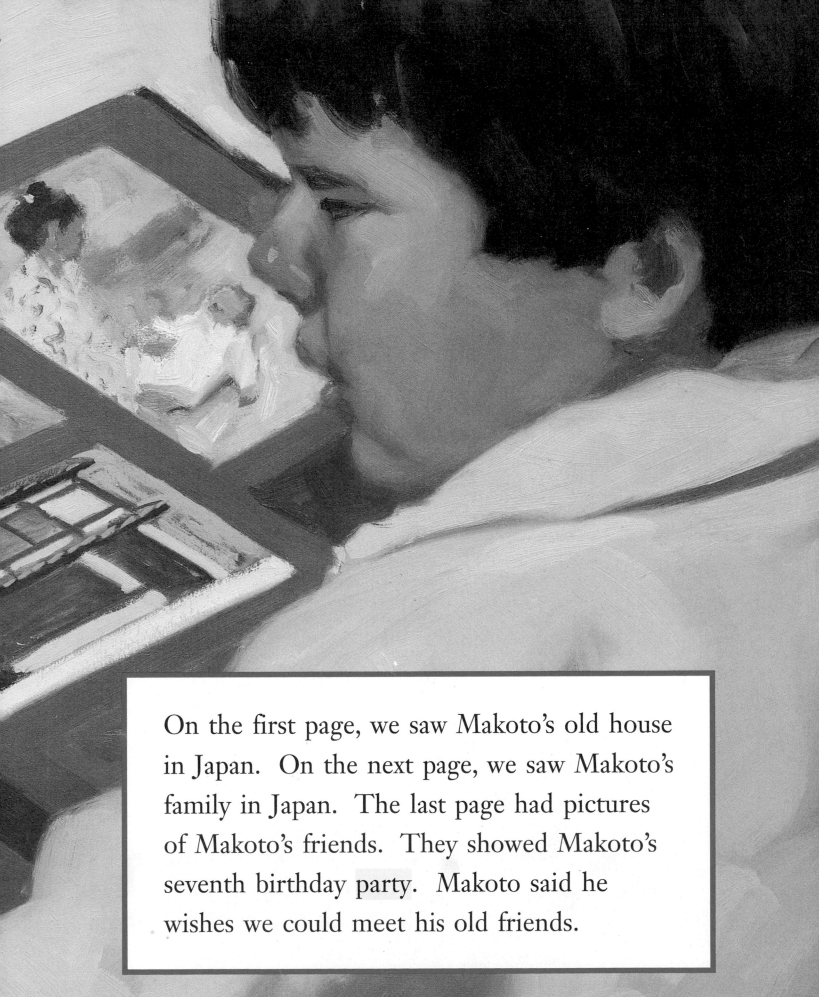

On the first page, we saw Makoto's old house in Japan. On the next page, we saw Makoto's family in Japan. The last page had pictures of Makoto's friends. They showed Makoto's seventh birthday party. Makoto said he wishes we could meet his old friends.

At the end of the day, Makoto's mother and
father repaid us for helping—with cookies!
We said "please" and "thank you" and ate up.

Makoto's father said he had a new job in the
city. Makoto would be going to our school.
We were all glad about that!

ANALYZE THE TEXT

Understanding Characters
What are Makoto's parents
like? Use text evidence and
the pictures.

We said good-bye to Makoto and his
mother and father. Then we went
home to our families. We were glad
to have a new friend next door.

Dig Deeper

Read Together

How to Analyze the Text

Use these pages to learn about Understanding Characters and the Narrator. Then read **The New Friend** again.

Understanding Characters

You read about a **character** named Makoto in **The New Friend**. Think about what Makoto says and does in the story. You can use these clues, or text evidence, to figure out how he feels and what he is like. List clues about Makoto and the other characters to help you understand them better. Use a chart like this one.

Words	Actions	Feelings

RL.1.3 describe characters, settings, and major events; **RL.1.6** identify who is telling the story; **RL.1.7** use illustrations and details to describe characters, setting, or events

COMMON CORE

Go Digital

Narrator

Sometimes a character tells the story. This character is the **narrator**. The narrator may use words like **I**, **me**, and **we**.

Which character in **The New Friend** do you think is telling the story? Why do you think so? Look for text evidence in the words and pictures to help you figure it out.

Your Turn

RETURN TO THE ESSENTIAL QUESTION

 **Turn and Talk**

What can you learn from someone who is from another country?

What do you think the boys in the story will learn from Makoto? Describe how the boys and Makoto feel about each other. Use text evidence.

 Classroom Conversation

Talk about these questions with your class.

1. How do you think Makoto feels about moving to a new place?

2. What are Makoto's new friends like?

3. How would you make a new friend feel welcome?

Response Read pages 170–171 again. What do you learn about Makoto? Use evidence from the words and pictures in the story for more clues about what Makoto is like. Write sentences to tell your opinion of Makoto. Give reasons.

Writing Tip

Your last sentence should be a nice ending. It can tell your opinion again.

COMMON CORE **RL.1.1** ask and answer questions about key details; **RL.1.3** describe characters, settings, and major events; **RL.1.7** use illustrations and details to describe characters, setting, or events; **W.1.1** write opinion pieces; **SL.1.4** describe people, places, things, and events with details/express ideas and feelings clearly

INFORMATIONAL TEXT

Read Together

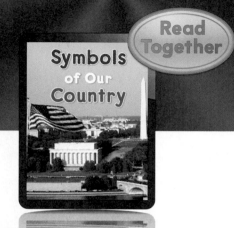

Symbols of Our Country

✓ GENRE

Informational text gives facts about a topic. It can be a newspaper, magazine, or textbook. Read to find facts about symbols of our country.

✓ TEXT FOCUS

Headings are titles for different parts of a selection. They tell what the section is about. What headings do you see in this selection? What information do they give?

COMMON CORE **RI.1.5** know and use text features to locate facts or information; **RI.1.10** read informational texts

Go Digital

Symbols of Our Country

by Agatha Jane

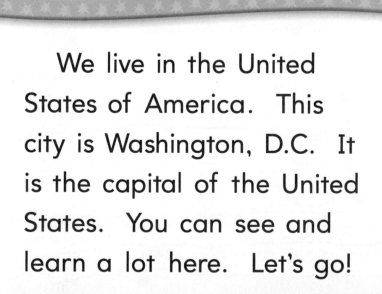

We live in the United States of America. This city is Washington, D.C. It is the capital of the United States. You can see and learn a lot here. Let's go!

American Flag

The flag is a symbol of the United States. The red and white stripes stand for the first thirteen states. The stars stand for each state that is part of the United States now.

Washington Monument

George Washington was our first President. This tall building is named for him. This painting of George Washington is in the White House.

Lincoln Memorial

Abraham Lincoln was our sixteenth President. You can see his statue at the Lincoln Memorial.

White House

The President works and lives here. People from all states vote for the person they want to be President.

Capitol Building

Voters from each state elect people to represent them. This is where they make laws.

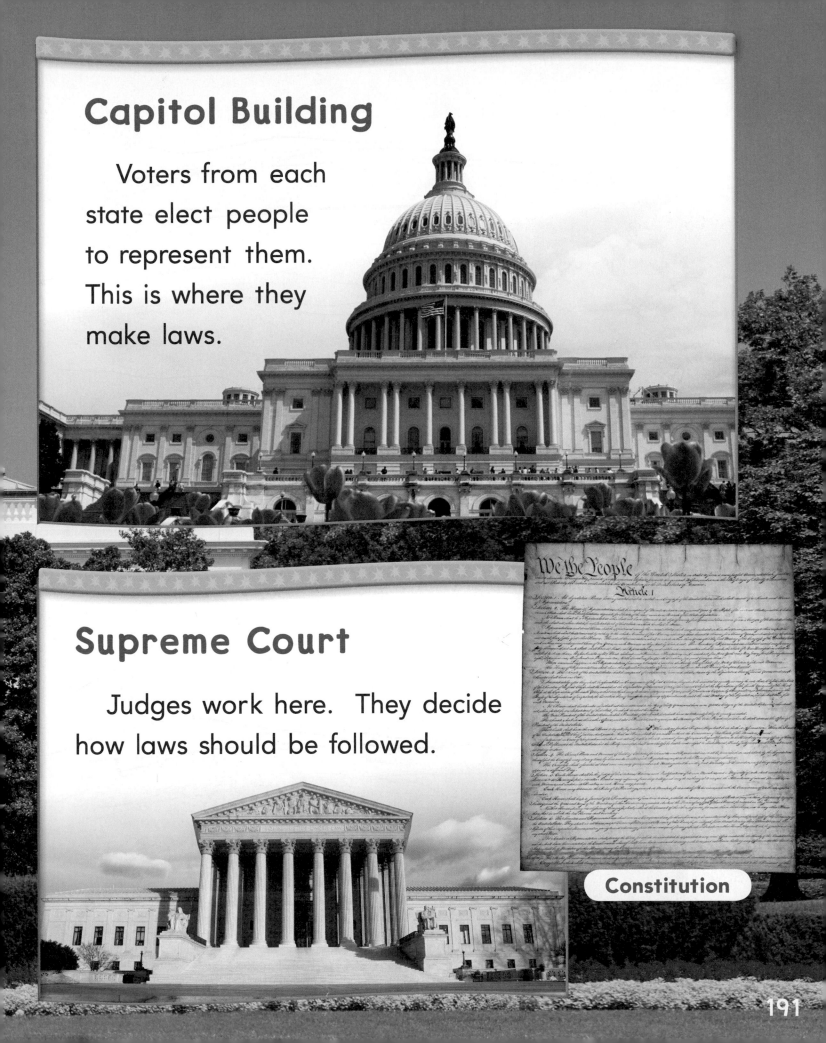

Supreme Court

Judges work here. They decide how laws should be followed.

Constitution

Mount Rushmore

You can see symbols of our country all over the United States. We are very proud of our country!

Liberty Bell

Statue of Liberty

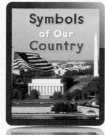

Compare Texts

Read Together

TEXT TO TEXT

Look it Up What country is Makoto's family from? Find out about that country's flag. Find out about other symbols of that country.

TEXT TO SELF

Describe a Symbol What American symbol do you like best? Tell what it looks like. Give reasons why you like it.

TEXT TO WORLD

Connect to Social Studies What changes happen when people move to a new country? What stays the same? Talk with a group.

Go Digital

COMMON CORE

RI.1.1 ask and answer questions about key details; **RI.1.3** describe the connection between individuals, events, ideas, or information in a text; **SL.1.1b** build on others' talk in conversations by responding to others' comments; **SL.1.4** describe people, places, things, and events with details/express ideas and feelings clearly

RF.1.3b decode regularly spelled one-syllable words; **L.1.1d** use personal, possessive, and indefinite pronouns; **L.1.2d** use conventional spelling for words with common spelling patterns and for frequently occurring irregular words

Grammar

Contractions A **contraction** is a short way of writing two words. This mark (') takes the place of missing letters. It is called an **apostrophe**.

It is a very big truck! It's a very big truck!
He is helping his dad. He's helping his dad.
This box **is not** too heavy. This box isn't too heavy.
I **do not** know what is in it. I **don't** know what is in it.

Read each sentence. Write the contraction for the underlined words. Use another sheet of paper.

1. <u>I am</u> happy to meet a new friend.

2. Today <u>he is</u> moving next door.

3. Jamal <u>is not</u> finished unpacking.

4. I <u>do not</u> know what games he likes.

5. His toys <u>are not</u> on the shelves yet.

 Grammar in Writing

When you proofread your writing, be sure you have written contractions correctly.

W.1.3 write narratives; **W.1.5** focus on a topic, respond to questions/suggestions from peers, and add details to strengthen writing; **L.1.1j** produce and expand simple and compound declarative, interrogative, imperative, and exclamatory sentences

Reading-Writing Workshop: **Revise**

Narrative Writing

✓ **Sentence Fluency** A good **story** usually has some short sentences and some long ones. Deval drafted a story about two friends. Later, he made a long sentence by joining two short sentences with **and**.

Revised Draft

Burt picked a bunch of
apples. , and He packed them up.

Revising Checklist

✓ Did I write some short and long sentences?

✓ Does my story have a beginning, a middle, and an ending?

✓ Did I write the exact words a character says?

✓ Did I use time-order words?

Find short and long sentences in Deval's story. Use the Checklist to revise your own draft.

Best Friends

Burt and Al lived in a beehive. They were best friends. They both flew fast. They both liked apples. Then Al moved south where there were no apples. Al called Burt. "I'm so sad," he said. Soon they had an idea. Burt picked a bunch of apples, and he packed them up. Then he got on a jet. When Burt got to Al's house, Al was so happy! The friends had juicy apples to celebrate.

Read the story and the article. As you read, stop and answer each question. Use text evidence.

An Old Friend

Tadpole and Fish are friends. They like to swim in the pond. One day, Fish goes out to look for Tadpole. She cannot find him. She is very upset.

---

1 Retell what has happened so far. Why is Fish upset?

The weeks pass by. Fish swims all by herself. She misses being with her friend, Tadpole.

COMMON CORE **RL.1.1** ask and answer questions about key details; **RL.1.2** retell stories and demonstrate understanding of the message or lesson; **RL.1.3** describe characters, settings, and major events; **RL.1.9** compare and contrast adventures and experiences of characters; **RL.1.10** read prose and poetry; **RI.1.1** ask and answer questions about key details; **RI.1.2** identify the main topic and retell key details;

One day, Fish hears a big PLOP! A frog swims up to her.

"Fish!" the frog says. "I was looking for you."

"Do I know you?" Fish asks.

"Yes," says the frog. "I am your old friend, Tadpole. Now I am a frog. I grew up!"

"I missed you!" says Fish. "I am glad you found me, Frog."

---

2 What happened to Tadpole that did not happen to Fish?

RI.1.3 describe the connection between individuals, events, ideas, or information in a text; **RI.1.7** use illustrations and details to describe key ideas; **RI.1.10** read informational texts

199

Butterfly Visitors

Each fall, monarch butterflies fly south to Mexico. They go there for the winter because it is warm. It can be a long, long trip. The butterflies stop to rest in towns along the way.

> ❸ Why do the butterflies fly south?

Some towns have a big party when the butterflies come! People dress up in orange and black. These are the colors of the butterflies. The people dance and sing. They are happy to see the butterflies!

People put tags on some of the butterflies. This helps keep track of them. We can learn more about the long trip each butterfly takes.

> ❹ What is this article mainly about?
> What facts did you learn?

Unit 5   High-Frequency Words

㉑ The Garden

few	window
loudly	story
noise	shall
night	world

㉔ A Tree Is a Plant

kinds	earth
country	almost
warms	ready
soil	covers

㉒ Amazing Animals

learning	young
begins	follow
until	years
eight	baby

㉕ The New Friend

city	seven
myself	buy
school	please
party	family

㉓ Whistle for Willie

house	father
along	again
together	nothing
boy	began

Glossary

A

adult

An **adult** is a grown-up. A crossing guard is often an **adult** who helps children cross a busy street.

amazing

Something **amazing** will cause surprise. It is **amazing** to see a shooting star.

B

blossoms

A **blossom** is a small flower on a tree or plant. The pink cherry **blossoms** will fall and then cherries will grow.

brushes

A **brush** is a tool that is used for scrubbing. We use the **brushes** to scrub the floors.

C

camel

A **camel** is a large animal with a long neck and one or two humps. We saw a **camel** at the animal park.

candles

A **candle** is made of wax, and a string in the middle is burned for light. When the electricity went off, we lit **candles** to help us see.

carton

A **carton** is a box used to store things. Martin packed his toys in the **carton** before he moved.

center

The **center** of something is the middle. There is a pit in the **center** of a peach.

color

A **color** is a kind of light that comes from an object to our eyes. Green is my favorite **color**.

crates

A **crate** is a kind of box used for packing things. We packed the books in **crates** to move them.

crew

A **crew** is a group of people who work together.
The **crew** worked together to build the ship.

D

dolphin

A **dolphin** is a sea animal related
to a whale. The **dolphin** swam
next to the ship.

E

empty

Empty means with nothing inside. When I opened the
box, it was **empty**.

errand

An **errand** is a short trip you take to do something.
I ran an **errand** for my mom.

F

frightened

To be **frightened** means to be scared. My dog is **frightened** by thunderstorms.

G

grocery

A **grocery** store is where you buy food. Luke stopped at the **grocery** store to pick up some bread for dinner.

H

happened

To **happen** means to take place. Mr. Chow read about what **happened** in the park.

hundreds

One **hundred** is a number that is one more than ninety-nine. The term **"hundreds"** means very many. There must be hundreds of ants in that big anthill!

O

of course

The words **of course** mean that something is expected to happen. It's lunchtime, and so **of course** we'll have lunch.

P

pails

A **pail** is something you use to carry things. The people used **pails** to carry water to put out the fire.

pocket

A **pocket** is a small bag of cloth. I always keep my money in the **pocket** of my pants.

poems

A **poem** is a kind of writing that often has rhyming words and rhythm. I will write funny **poems** about driving a car to a star and swimming in the sea with a big bee.

polar bear

A **polar bear** is a large white bear that lives where it is cold. A **polar bear** will roll in the snow to clean its fur.

porcupine

A **porcupine** is an animal that is covered with long sharp quills. Most animals will leave a **porcupine** alone.

R

rejoined

To **rejoin** means to get together again. We **rejoined** the group after we finished our chores.

repaid

To **repay** means to give something back. I **repaid** my brother the money he loaned me.

S

seventh
If something is **seventh**, that means that there are six things before it. Saturday is the **seventh** day of the week.

shadow
A **shadow** is a dark area with light around it. The sun made a **shadow** behind the tree.

shouted
When you **shout**, you speak very loudly. When we won the game, everyone **shouted**, "Hooray!"

soccer
Soccer is a game where players kick a ball. Nina was a very good **soccer** player because she was fast.

staked
To **stake** means to use a pointed stick to help something stand up. Andrea **staked** the plant to help it grow straight.

stroked

To **stroke** means to rub gently. Matt **stroked** the puppy to make it calm down.

T

themselves

Themselves means those people or animals. As animals get older, they can take care of **themselves**.

toes

Toes are the parts of the foot that help people and animals walk. People have five **toes** on each foot.

U

unloaded
To **unload** means to take off or take out. The woman **unloaded** the bags of food from the car.

unpack
To **unpack** means to take out of a box or a suitcase. We started to **unpack** the boxes in the kitchen.

W

whirled
To **whirl** means to spin or to turn in circles. My little brother **whirled** and whirled until he was dizzy.

Acknowledgments

"Caballito blanco, reblanco/Little White Horse" from *Mamá Goose: A Latino Nursery Treasury* by Alma Flor Ada and F. Isabel Campoy. Text copyright ©2004 by Alma Flor Ada and F. Isabel Campoy. Reprinted by permission of Hyperion Books for Children. All rights reserved.

"The Garden" from *Frog and Toad Together* by Arnold Lobel. Copyright ©1971 by Arnold Lobel. Reprinted by permission of HarperCollins Publishers.

The New Friend, originally published as *El Amigo Nuevo* by Maria Puncel, illustrated by Ulises Wensell. Copyright ©1995 Laredo Publishing Company. Reprinted by permission of Laredo Publishing Company, Inc.

"Pet Snake" by Rebecca Kai Dotlich from *A Pet For Me*, published by HarperCollins. Copyright ©2003 by Rebecca Kai Dotlich. Reprinted by permission of Curtis Brown, Ltd.

A Tree Is a Plant by Clyde Robert Bulla, illustrated by Stacey Schuett. Text copyright ©1960 by Clyde Robert Bulla. Illustrations copyright ©2001 by Stacey Schuett. Reprinted by permission of HarperCollins Publishers.

Whistle for Willie by Ezra Jack Keats. Copyright ©1964 by Ezra Jack Keats. All rights reserved including the right of reproduction in whole or in part in any form. Reprinted by permission of Viking Children's Books, a member of Penguin Young Readers Group, a division of Penguin Group (USA), Inc.

Credits

Placement Key:
(r) right, (l) left, (c) center, (t) top, (b) bottom, (bg) background

Photo Credits
3 (cl) imagebroker / Alamy; 3 (cl) © Bon Appetit / Alamy; 3 (cl) © Trevor Smithers ARPS / Alamy; 4 (cl) ©Design Pics Inc./John Pitcher/Alamy Images; 4 ©Purestock/Alamy Images; 4 (cl) Byron Jorjorian/Digital Vision/Getty Images; 4 ©Photodisc/Getty Images; 6 (l) ©Patrick Bernard/Getty Images; 6 (cl) Ariel Skelley/Getty Images; 7 (cl) © Hoberman Collection / Alamy;

Blind [9] ©GK Hart/Vikki Hart/Stone/Getty Images; 10 ©Radius Images/Getty Images; 10 (cr) ©Gary Crabbe/Alamy; 10 (tc) imagebroker / Alamy; 10 (tc) © Bon Appetit / Alamy; 10 (tc) © Trevor Smithers ARPS / Alamy; 11 ©William Leaman/Alamy Images; 11 Corbis; 11 (br) ©Scott Barrow/Corbis; 11 (tr) ©Mark Bolton/Corbis; 11 (bl) ©Comstock /SuperStock; 11 (cl) ©John Henley/Corbis; 12 Ros Drinkwater / Alamy; 12 ©Katrina Brown/Alamy Images; 31 © MBI / Alamy; 34 (bg) © Bon Appetit / Alamy; 34 (tl) imagebroker / Alamy; 34 (tl) © Bon Appetit / Alamy; 34 (tl) © Trevor Smithers ARPS / Alamy; 35 (l) imagebroker / Alamy; 35 (r) © Trevor Smithers ARPS / Alamy; 36 (bg) © CuboImages srl / Alamy; 36 (t) Photo Researchers/Getty Images; 36 (b) imagebroker / Alamy; 37 Wealan Pollard/Getty Images; 37 ©Oote Boe Photography/Alamy Images; 37 (tc) imagebroker / Alamy; 37 (tc) © Bon Appetit / Alamy; 37 (tc) © Trevor Smithers ARPS / Alamy; 42 (tl) ©Design Pics Inc./John Pitcher/Alamy Images; 42 (br) ©Brand X Pictures/Getty Images; 42 (c) ©A & M SHAH/Animals Animals - Earth Scenes; 42 (tl) Byron Jorjorian/Digital Vision/Getty Images; 42 (tl) ©Photodisc/Getty Images; 43 (tl) ©Design Pics Inc./Richard Wear/Alamy Images; 43 (tl) ©Design Pics Inc./Richard Wear/Alamy Images; 43 (cl) ©Beverly Joubert/National Geographic/ Getty Images; 43 (br) © Keren Su/China Span/ Alamy; 43 (tr) ©Blickwinkel/Alamy Images; 43 (bl) ©DLILLC/Corbis; 43 (cr) ©Gavriel Jecan/ Photographer's Choice/Getty Images; 44 ©Design Pics Inc./John Pitcher/Alamy Images; 44 Byron Jorjorian/Digital Vision/Getty Images; 44 (bg) ©Photodisc/Getty Images; 45 Travel Pictures / Alamy; 46 (tl) ©Design Pics Inc./John Pitcher/ Alamy Images; 46 ©Photodisc/Getty Images; 46 (br) ©Paul Hanna/Reuters/Corbis; 46 (tl) Byron Jorjorian/Digital Vision/Getty Images; 46 ©Photodisc/Getty Images; 47 ©Design Pics Inc./ John Pitcher/Alamy Images; 47 Byron Jorjorian/ Digital Vision/Getty Images; 48 (tl) ©Just One Film/The Image Bank/Getty Images; 48 ©Design Pics Inc./John Pitcher/Alamy Images; 48 (inset) ©Just One Film/The Image Bank/Getty Images; 48 (r) ©GK Hart/Vikki Hart/The Image Bank/ Getty Images; 48 (br) ©Paul Hanna/Reuters/ Corbis; 49 ©Design Pics Inc./John Pitcher/Alamy Images; 50 (l) ©David Trood/Getty Images;